SEA WOLVES

In a wrinkle of the rugged coast
where the forest drops
       into the sea
a quiet cove holds secrets
       for those
              who look close
                     wade in
                     breathe deep . . .

SEA WOLVES

KEEPERS OF THE RAINFOREST

BY MEGAN BENEDICT AND MELANIE CROWDER   ART BY ROY HENRY VICKERS

ASTRA YOUNG READERS

AN IMPRINT OF ASTRA BOOKS FOR YOUNG READERS

New York

Waves spill over tangled kelp
and discarded shells,
   fill a trail of paw prints—
      tiny wells that sift
   and still the water.

The hunt has moved on.
Claw-pricks fade—
one more wave
and all trace will be gone.

Gray skies drip rain
into steel-gray sea:

plink—

                plink—

      drops sink
     into thick fur
damp and matted with salt.

Rippling bodies slide between tides
paddle across inlets
wavelets,
braving murky depths
and lurking swimmers far below.

The strong ones know
they must
bring enough
home.

On the distant shore
wet snouts explore tide pools
in full bloom.

Nestled in rocks the color of fur,
the color of sky and sea,
  clams are wrenched free
    cracked with sharp teeth

slurp—

            smack—

    a salty snack, then
    retreat before the tide comes back.

Beyond the bay, the river awaits
a tumble of scales
and shimmering tails

plunge—

snap—

a mouthful of pink meat,
tasty dinner treat.

They slip ashore,
and back once more along
        the forest floor, overgrown
green and moss-soft.

Hackles lift
ears prick, tick toward
the roar

whirr—

crunch—

of beastly metal saws
and crushing steely claws.

Rumble-throat worry,
　　silent-slink
　　　　—hurry.

A howl lifts delicate leaves
circles crumpled trees and blunted trunks
　rises over the cacophony,
　　calling the roaming
　　　distant ones,
　singing the pack home.

Red-tipped ghosts
        lope through a sea of ferns,
    circle well-worn turns
into the thick of the woods.

Beneath a twisted cedar root
shadows shift, ears lift . . .

. . . pups tumble out, all
wet-snout hellos
and hungry-belly yips.

Soon they will be the hunters,
the sleek river runners,
open water seekers,
sacred keepers
of the rainforest.

Not Your Average Wolf

When you think of wolves, what do you see?

You probably don't imagine beachcombers, tide-pool foragers, or wet-eared swimmers paddling between islands. But the sea wolves of western Canada and southeastern Alaska are exactly that.

These wolves are often smaller and tend to have shorter, coarser, red-tinted fur compared to interior wolves. Though scientists are just beginning to learn about this amazing coastal form of the gray wolf family, Indigenous peoples have long known of their unique way of life and respected their vital roles in the ecosystem.

They eat seafood.

Living the island life has changed more than just their fur. While sea wolves do eat deer like their inland cousins, they often pick seafood instead. They scavenge beached whales, hunt seals, and swipe salmon from rivers. When the tide is low, it's a buffet! They slurp fish eggs from kelp fronds, gnaw on mussels and barnacles, pry open clams, and catch skittering crabs.

They swim!

If you're picturing a dog paddle, you're not far off. When sea wolves swim between islands, only their heads are visible above the water. Because so much of their diet is found in or near the ocean, they don't have to spread out across their entire territory as most wolves do. Instead, they tend to stick to the coastlines, often island-hopping to find food. Amazingly, these wolves have been recorded swimming almost eight miles at a time!

It takes a family . . .

It's a lot of work to raise a litter of wolf pups! During the spring, two to ten pups per litter begin life in an old-growth forest, born in a den, which is often safely tucked under the roots of a large tree. At first, the pups are blind and deaf and rely on their mother's milk. Mama needs help, so other members of the family bring her food while she cares for her young. After three weeks, the pups can eat some of this regurgitated meat which has been chewed, swallowed, stored in the stomach, and then spit back up again. One or two family members take turns babysitting while the pups start playing outside the den, and the mother joins in the hunt. When the pups become juveniles, their eyes turn from blue to gold, and the family moves out of the den to a rendezvous site, often a spot with access to plentiful food. In the shallow mouth of the river, where fishing is easy, the pups learn to catch salmon and eat the heads to fatten up for the coming winter. They will remain with the group for two to three years, after which some will leave to start families of their own.

Keepers of the Rainforest

The cool, temperate rainforests rely on sea wolves, apex predators at the top of the food chain. After they catch salmon and eat the heads, the wolves often leave the rest of the carcass, which becomes food for smaller scavengers and eventually decomposes on the riverbank and in the forest. The marine nutrients from the fish nourish plants and trees, helping the entire ecosystem to thrive. Additionally, without wolves, there would be too many deer, who then clear the forest of groundcover, home to many small animals and the next generation of towering trees.

For many years, humans have threatened the survival of this magnificent species. Climate change has shifted weather patterns and season lengths and caused variations in ocean levels. This makes it hard to find food. Logging destroys old-growth forests, the habitat for both the sea wolves and their prey, and sadly, wolves are too often killed by people who don't understand how important they are.

Now that you do—*you* can help! Share what you know about these elusive animals and together we can protect them and their habitat. The rainforest and all the creatures in this complex coastal web of life depend on the sea wolves. And their survival is up to all of us.

—Megan Benedict and Melanie Crowder

Sea Wolves in My Life

I come from a small ancient village on the Pacific Northwest coast called, Kitkatla, spelled, Gitxaala these days. My home village is over five thousand years old. My ancestors learned to exist on this coast for thousands of generations by observing nature. The wolf, the orca, the eagle, and the raven are the four clans of our village.

I grew up with sea wolves as they are called today. I've enjoyed their conversations and had them answer me as I howled like a wolf. I've seen their tracks in the sand many times and knew they were close by. I learned not to be afraid of them and observed their quiet and gentle ways.

There's one story I heard from my uncle who was out hunting for seals. They were approaching one of their favorite rocks where they knew seals liked to rest. We always hunt seals by boat. As they were approaching the seal rock, they noticed a log that was moving against the current toward the same rock. As they watched, they saw this log stop, and five wolves appeared from behind the log. They were amazed that the wolves were using the log to sneak up to the rock and the seals. This story illustrates how clever our coastal wolves are.

One day near Tofino, British Columbia, where I have my art gallery, I was out in my boat jigging cod and feeding eagles. After enjoying the eagles, I stopped in a bay to enjoy lunch. In the quiet of the bay, I heard the howl of a wolf so I answered with my howl. The wolf howled back, and I knew it must be close so I scanned the beach and there, on a little rocky point, I saw this young wolf sitting. I howled and could see it howl back. An incredible feeling of being accepted filled me. Eventually other wolves howled from the forest and the little one left the beach, walking into the forest.

As our ancestors did, we learned to hunt deer on islands in a group like a wolf family. A group of us boys would start at one end of an island and move to the other side in a line, making lots of noise to frighten the deer. The deer would reach the other end of the island and start swimming to another island close by. The men in our village would use ropes to catch the deer. The deer would be gathered up and taken back to the village for food.

There are many stories of wolves that I recall. Another that comes to mind is a canoe trip I was on early one foggy morning. I slipped through the water quietly and enjoyed watching life around me. I came into this large bay with a big beach because the tide was low. This is when wolves walk the beaches looking for clams, cockles, or crabs. I heard this almost lonesome long howl coming from the foggy beach and stopped paddling to listen. I then heard the howl of a wolf pup; it sounded so cute. My eyes strained toward the sounds. I wanted to see the wolves. They appeared faintly as gray forms in the fog, and I was privileged to watch mother and cub howling. It was as though she were teaching her pup.

Our people are called Git Lax Moen, which can be interpreted as "People of the Salt Waters." Wolves of the sea have been a part of our lives for thousands of years.

—Roy Henry Vickers

For Jesse, who has been with me every step
of this journey —*MB*

For Camden Henry —*MC*

I dedicate my work in *Sea Wolves* to my people
of Gitxaala, where sea wolves are experienced to
this day —*RHV*

Acknowledgment
The publisher thanks Chris Darimont of the University of Victoria, British
Columbia, Canada, for his careful review of the text. Dr. Darimont has
volunteered for twenty-five years with the Raincoast Conservation
Foundation, a science-based nonprofit organization that started the first
and only research on Canada's sea wolves and that works to protect them.
You can learn more about their work at raincoast.org.

Astra Young Readers
An imprint of Astra Books for Young Readers,
a division of Astra Publishing House
astrapublishinghouse.com
Printed in China

ISBN: 978-1-6626-2011-9 (hc)
ISBN: 978-1-6626-2012-6 (eBook)
Library of Congress Control Number: 2023921001

First edition

10 9 8 7 6 5 4 3 2 1

Design by Barbara Grzeslo
The text is set in Neutraface Demi.
The illustrations are done digitally.